☆ American Girl®

ULTIMATE STICKER COLLECTION

Dress up

How to use this book

Read the captions, then find the sticker that best fits the space.
(Hint: check the bold sticker labels for clues!)

•

There are lots of fantastic extra stickers for creating
your own scenes throughout the book.

DK | Penguin Random House

Written and edited by Eleanor Rose
Designed by Lisa Sodeau, Jaynan Spengler,
and Jade Wheaton

First American Edition, 2017
Published in the United States by DK Publishing
1450 Broadway, New York, New York 10018

Page design copyright © 2017 Dorling Kindersley Limited
DK, a division of Penguin Random House LLC

21 22 19 18 17 16 15 14 13
013–298003–02/2017

A catalog record for this book is available from
the Library of Congress.

ISBN: 978-1-4654-5690-8

DK books are available at special discounts when
purchased in bulk for sales promotions, premiums,
fund-raising, or educational use. For details, contact:
DK Publishing Special Markets, 1450 Broadway,
New York, New York 10018
SpecialSales@dk.com

Printed and bound in China

www.americangirl.com

A WORLD OF IDEAS:
SEE ALL THERE IS TO KNOW

www.dk.com

Standout style

Each BeForever™ character has her own individual style. The one thing they all have in common is that they always look super-stylish!

Groovy vest

❧ 1974 ❧

Flower power
Julie's style is far-out!
She loves bright colors,
flower patterns, and cool
braids in her hair.

Bell-bottom jeans

Platform sandals

Hair ties

❧ 1764 ❧

Little details
Kaya's dress has lots of pretty fringing, beads, and a tie belt. Her moccasins keep her feet warm and dry.

Cloche hat

Fringed dress

❧ 1934 ❧

Dress to impress
Kit's ready for a day out in her charming floral dress. The matching bracelet, hat, and bag finish the look.

Flowery dress

Red strappy shoes

3

All dressed up

The girls love special occasions. Whether it's a family feast, a day out, or a trip to church, they can't wait to put on their best outfits.

Ruffled camisa (blouse)

❧ 1824 ❧

Feast outfit

Josefina™ wears this special outfit for the feast of San José. Her white camisa goes perfectly with her turquoise skirt.

Embroidered skirt

Satin slippers

Hair bow

⪻ 1904 ⪼

City style

Samantha™ wears this pink, ruffled dress on a special trip to New York City. She looks great in the fashionable city!

Brimmed hat

Purple-print dress

Ruffled dress

Lavender boots

Button boots

⪻ 1864 ⪼

Sunday best

Addy™ loves the purple dress that Momma made for her. She wears it to church on Sundays with her matching hat.

5

Favorite things

A pretty dress, a choir outfit, or a costume for an onstage performance—each of the girls has a special outfit for her favorite hobby.

Ribbon hair bow

Dress with lace trim

Burgundy patent shoes

1904

Picture-perfect
Samantha™ enjoys painting outside. Her lace-trimmed flower dress and hair bow reflect her love of nature.

1964

Singing dress
Melody™ loves singing! Every week she puts on her favorite flowered dress and adds her voice to the church choir.

White gloves

Ruffled floral dress

Dress with shawl

Shiny shoes

1914

Stage style
Rebecca™ loves her theater costume. The pearly necklace, knitted shawl, and long gloves make her look like a star.

Ribbon shoes

7

Winter warmers

In the wintertime, the girls put on their warmest clothes and wrap up against the cold. Out in the snow, they look snug and stylish!

1864

Winter wear
Addy's winter coat has a cute plaid trim. Her coat, hat, and boots keep her warm on the chilly walk to church.

Derby hat

Thick green coat

Practical winter shoes

Fluffy hat

Furry collar coat

1904

Fancy coat
Samantha™ feels like a sophisticated city girl in her white coat and matching hat. She's ready for fun in the snow!

Stocking hat

Winter shoes and tights

Skating dress

1954

Ice-skating
Maryellen's special dress and hat keep her warm while she goes ice-skating for the very first time.

Ice skates

9

Schooltime

The girls always make sure they look neat and tidy in the classroom. Knee-length skirts, bright colors, and shiny shoes are pretty and practical.

Hat with bow

Cropped jacket

⊰ 1934 ⊱

Pretty in pink
Kit™ wears this classic mix-and-match outfit to school. Her felt hat is the finishing touch.

A-line skirt

Double T-strap shoes

∞ 1974 ∞
Class style
Julie's colorful outfit
reflects her sunny
personality! Her tunic
top and berry pants
brighten up her
school day.

∞ 1954 ∞
School days
Maryellen™ wears a purple
gingham dress to school.
The Peter Pan collar and
black necktie make
it extra special.

Embroidered
tunic top

Gingham
dress

Flared
pants

Mary Jane shoes

Clogs

Sweet dreams

When the sun sets, it's time for the girls to get ready for bed. In their favorite pajamas, they are sure to have a good night's sleep.

Striped bow

1914

City sleep
Rebecca's pajamas are perfect for a cool night in her New York City apartment.

Pajama top

Shiny pants

Cool cotton

Josefina™ wears this cotton night shift to keep cool on warm evenings in New Mexico.

Night shift with ribbon

Patterned pajamas

Embroidered slippers

Perfect pajamas

Melody's blue slippers are decorated with cute pom-poms. Her braids keep her hair in place while she sleeps.

Pom-pom slippers

Accessorize

Cute accessories such as hats, bags, shoes, and belts add the perfect finishing touches to the girls' favorite outfits.

Pink corsage

~1954~

Birthday dress
Maryellen's excited to wear this beautiful dress with a pleated sash and corsage. It was a gift for her 10th birthday.

Shoes with bow

1964

Star style
Melody™ feels like a star in these cat-eye sunglasses! Her matching hat and bag complete her outfit.

Pillbox hat

Wide-brim sun hat

Shiny bag

Cropped vest

Knee-length socks

1824

Summer sun
Josefina™ wears this bright dress and vest on hot summer days. Her hat shades her face from the sun.

Use your extra stickers to fill the scene with your favorite dolls!

Meet Gabriela

Gabriela McBride™ can seem a little shy, but when she tames her stutter she has a lot to say. Through spoken-word poetry, Gabriela finds her voice.

Sequin top

Dance leggings

Sparkly shoes

Ready to perform
When performing onstage, Gabriela wears her sparkly top, shoes, and gloves to give her confidence an extra boost.

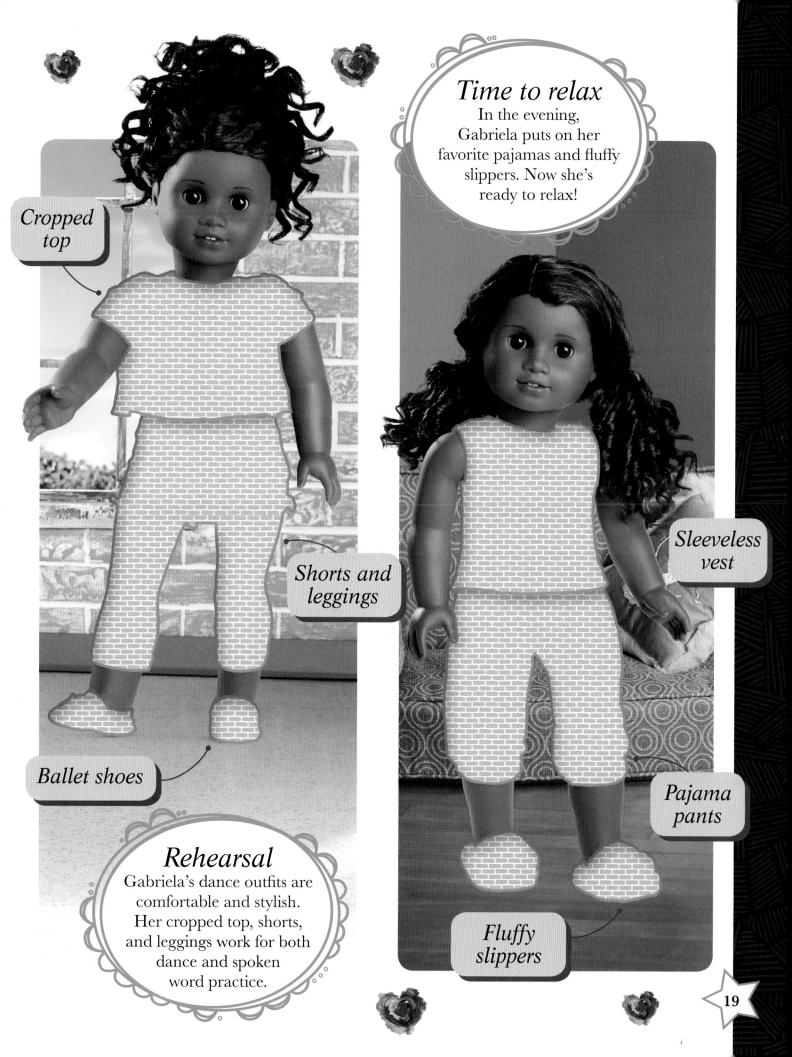

Cropped top

Time to relax
In the evening, Gabriela puts on her favorite pajamas and fluffy slippers. Now she's ready to relax!

Shorts and leggings

Sleeveless vest

Ballet shoes

Rehearsal
Gabriela's dance outfits are comfortable and stylish. Her cropped top, shorts, and leggings work for both dance and spoken word practice.

Pajama pants

Fluffy slippers

19

In the spotlight

For creative girls, there's nothing better than a fun-filled day of music and dancing! They choose outfits that will help them shine.

Music lesson
A sleeveless top, shorts, and sneakers make a comfortable and stylish outfit for a day of music practice.

Music book

Patterned top

Stage style
For guitar-loving girls, a cool jacket, skirt, and boots are the perfect rock star look.

Acoustic guitar

Black leotard

Knee-high boots

Tulle tutu

Ballet class
A budding ballerina looks just perfect in a black leotard, pretty pink tutu, and ribbon ballet shoes.

Ribbon ballet shoes

Outdoor fun

Every hobby needs a cool outfit to match. For girls who love to be outside, fresh air, fun, and fashionable clothes are the perfect combination.

Pink helmet

Horse riding

A pink horse-print scarf looks super-stylish paired with riding pants, a jacket, and boots. A pink helmet is cool and safe.

Riding jacket

Riding boots

Great outdoors
A warm hat, dress, and long boots make a cozy outfit for a night camping under the stars.

Cable-knit hat

Plaid dress

Soccer jersey

Long boots

On the field
A brightly colored uniform and the perfect soccer cleats make a star player look like a million dollars.

Soccer ball, cleats, and socks

Sleepover fun

What could be more fun than a sleepover with best friends? Games, giggles, and a pajama fashion show will make for a night to remember!

Top with two-tiered ruffle

Leopard-print shorts

Flip-flop slippers

Wild style
Mix and match a new look with this pretty frilly top and fuzzy leopard-print pajama bottoms.

Paisley-print top

Flower power
Bring the beauty of nature indoors with a paisley shirt and pretty slippers decorated with peacocks.

Cropped pajama pants

Cupcake top

Peacock slippers

Pink pajama pants

Cupcake slippers

Sweet dreams
With delicious decorations, these pajamas are perfect for a party. Cupcake slippers are the cherry on top.

25

Pretty extras

Whatever the weather or occasion, the perfect accessory can transform the girls' outfits from fine to fabulous in seconds!

Polka-dot umbrella

Stylish showers
A polka-dot umbrella with matching raincoat and rain boots can help the sun shine on a rainy day.

Bow rain boots

Summer sun
Bright colors are perfect for a sunny day. A yellow ruffled top looks great with blue shorts, a beach bag, and sun hat.

Straw sun hat

Headband

Beach bag

Waist bow

Purse with gem clasp

Beaded flip flops

Party dress
A pretty dress isn't complete without matching accessories! A headband, waist bow, and golden purse are just right.

Navy shoes

Dress-up fun

Whether it's for trick-or-treating at Halloween, or for a fun dress-up party, girls love to wear all kinds of cool costumes.

Head boppers

Buzzy bee

Yellow and black stripes make a beautiful bee costume! Sparkly wings and a head bopper totally transform the outfit.

Yellow-and-black tutu

Slip-on shoes

I WOOF U

Monster fun
A cobweb dress, "stitch" necklace, and a tall wig make a monstrously good costume!

Scary skeleton
A skeleton costume is perfect for Halloween trick-or-treating. A sparkly tutu adds a cute touch.

Skeleton T-shirt

Black-and-white wig

Lacy dress

Skeleton leggings

Pink sparkly shoes

Ankle boots

29

Winter style

Cold weather calls for lots of cozy layers. Have fun playing in the snow—and don't forget a touch of sparkle for the festive season!

Fluffy earmuffs

Turtleneck sweater

Snow fun
A winter's day needs a warm outfit. A thick sweater, quilted skirt, and fluffy boots are great for playing in the snow.

Sledding dogs

Sparkly headband

Party time
A golden dress is perfect for festive parties. Sequins will sparkle and shine under the bright lights.

Helmet and goggles

Sequin mini dress

Patterned ski jacket

Golden ankle strap shoes

Slope star
For style on the slopes, a colorful outfit is a must. A bright ski jacket and pants stand out from the crowd.

Skis

31

Use your extra stickers to fill the scene with your favorite dolls!

32

Groovy
vest

Bell-bottom
jeans

Platform sandals

Cloche hat

Hair ties

Flowery
dress

Fringed
dress

Red strappy
shoes

Embroidered skirt

Ruffled camisa (blouse)

Satin slippers

Hair bow

Brimmed hat

Ruffled dress

Purple-print dress

Lavender boots

Button boots

©/™ 2017 American Girl

Ribbon hair bow

Ruffled floral dress

Dress with lace trim

White gloves

Burgundy patent shoes

Shiny shoes

Dress with shawl

Jip

Scooter

Ribbon shoes

Stocking hat

Ice skates

Derby hat

Fluffy hat

Skating dress

Furry collar coat

Thick green coat

Practical winter shoes

Winter shoes and tights

Hat with bow

Cropped jacket

A-line skirt

Embroidered tunic top

Double T-strap shoes

Gingham dress

Flared pants

Julie's accessories

Mary Jane shoes

Clogs

Striped bow

Patterned pajamas

Pajama top

Gray kitten

Shiny pants

Pom-pom slippers

Night shift with ribbon

Julie's hairstyling set

Embroidered slippers

Terrier puppy

Melody's pajamas

©/™ 2017 American Girl

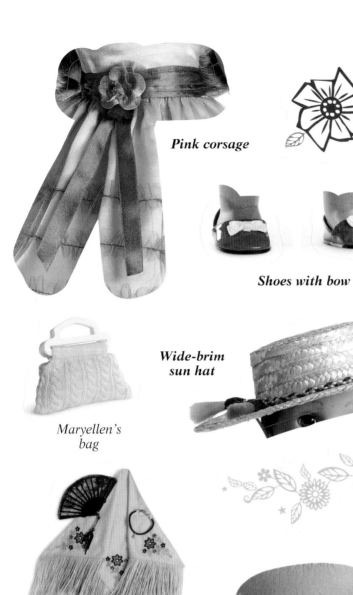
Pink corsage

Josefina's night shift

Shoes with bow

Wide-brim sun hat

Maryellen's bag

Cropped vest

Josefina's fan, shawl, and necklace

Pillbox hat

Shiny bag

Sombrita

Melody's hat

Kaya's necklace

Knee-length socks

Kaya's pouch

Josefina's boots

Sunglasses

Josefina's accessories

Rebecca's kittens

Sequin top

Dance leggings

Sparkly shoes

Sleeveless vest

IMAGINE DREAM CREATE

Cropped top

Shorts and leggings

Pajama pants

Fluffy slippers

Ballet shoes

Music book

Patterned top

Black leotard

Bracelets

Tulle tutu

Glasses

Acoustic guitar

Ribbon ballet shoes

Ballet dog

Pink ballet shoes

Pink leotard

Knee-high boots

Ballet skirt

Violin

©/™ 2017 American Girl

Pink helmet

Soccer jersey

Riding jacket

Soccer ball, cleats, and socks

Riding boots

Cable-knit hat

Sneakers

Plaid dress

Rain boots

Bucket hat

Long strap bag

Long boots

Top with two-tiered ruffle

Leopard-print shorts

Flip-flop slippers

Paisley-print top

Peacock slippers

Cropped pajama pants

Pink slippers

Cupcake top

Hairband

Cupcake slippers

Pink pajama pants

Comb

©/™ 2017 American Girl

Bow rain boots

Polka-dot umbrella

Purse with gem clasp

Headband

Straw sun hat

Navy shoes

Waist bow

Two-colour shoes

Beach bag

Box

Sun hat

Warm boots

Gem bracelet

Gold frame sunglasses

Beaded flip flops

Purple bag

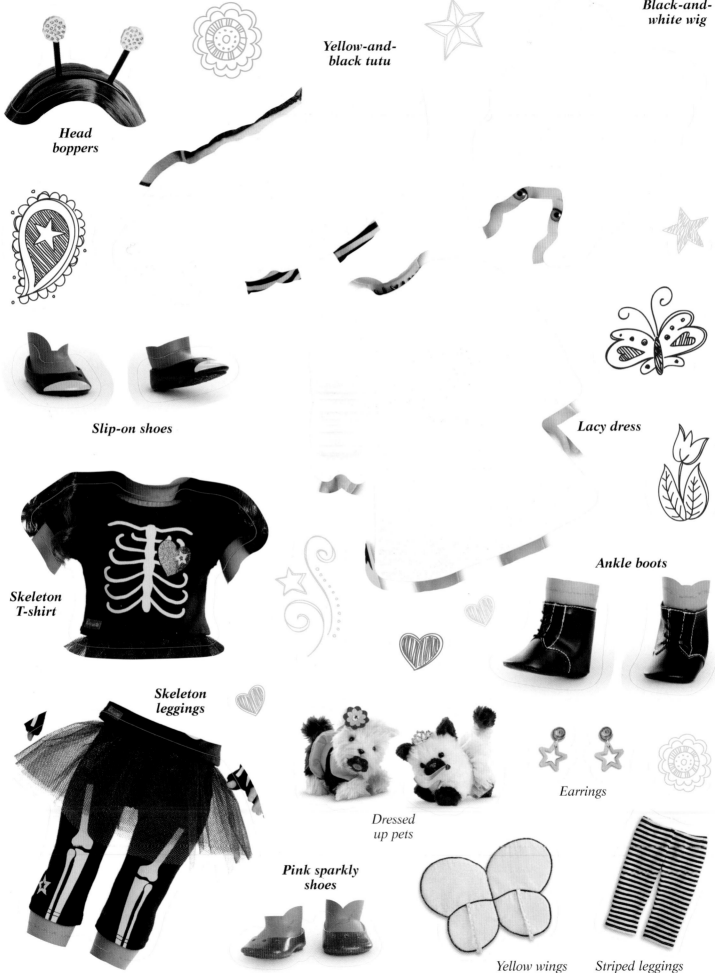

Head boppers

Yellow-and-black tutu

Black-and-white wig

Slip-on shoes

Lacy dress

Skeleton T-shirt

Ankle boots

Skeleton leggings

Dressed up pets

Earrings

Pink sparkly shoes

Yellow wings

Striped leggings

Fluffy
earmuffs

Turtleneck
sweater

Helmet and
goggles

Sledding
dogs

Patterned
ski jacket

Sequin
mini dress

Sparkly
headband

Skis

Golden ankle
strap shoes

©/™ 2017 American Girl

Extra Stickers

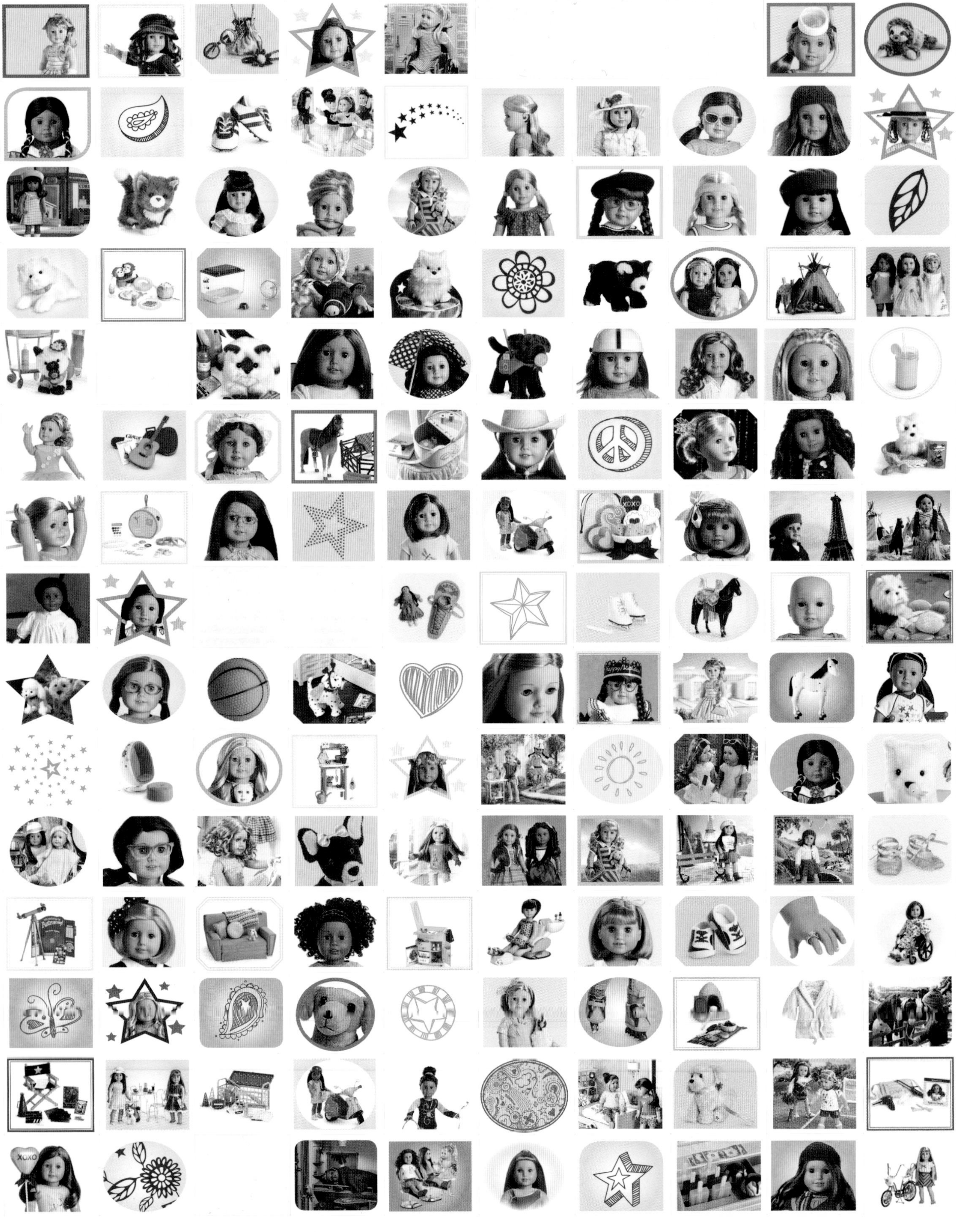

Extra Stickers

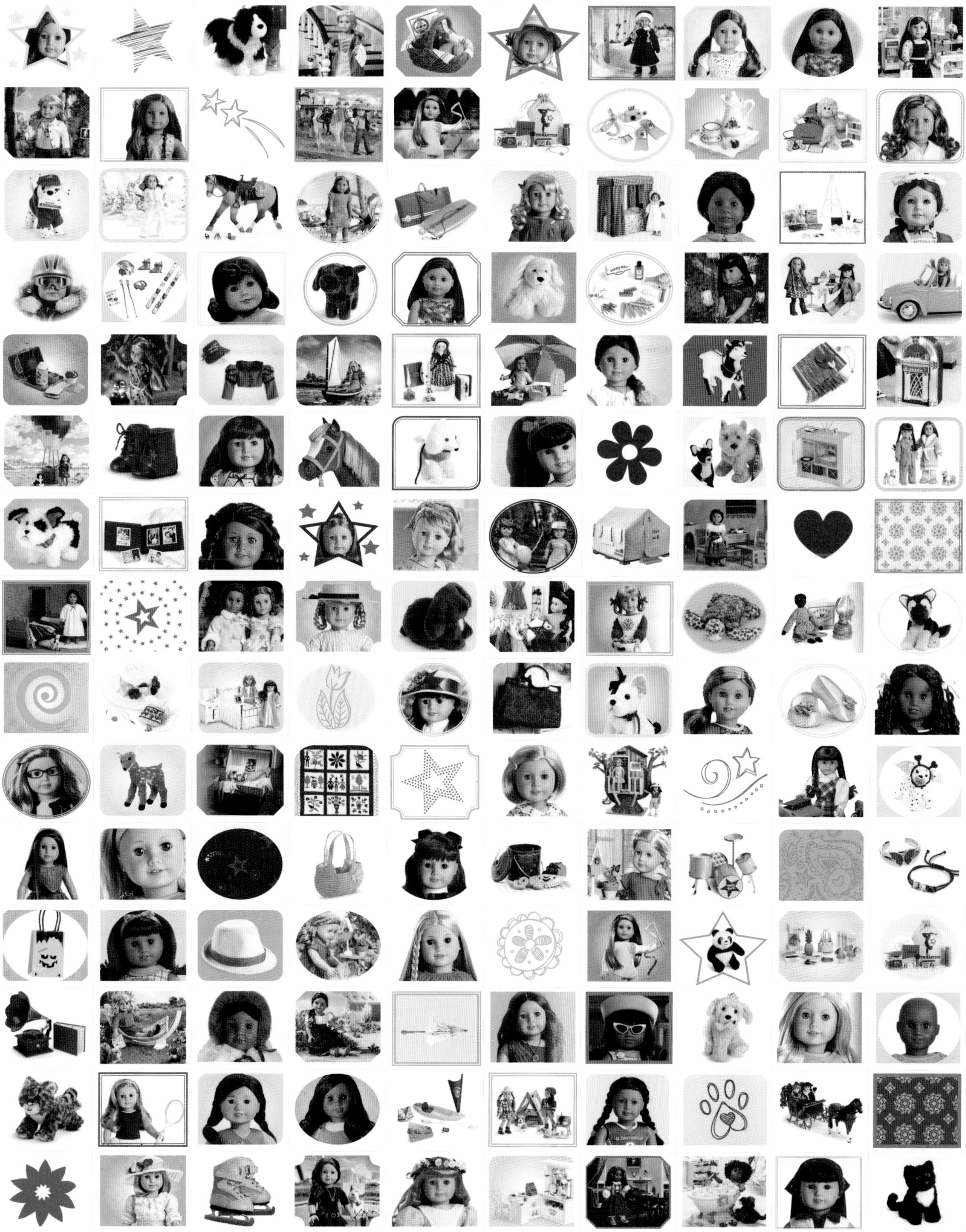

Extra Stickers

Extra Stickers

©/™ 2017 American Girl

Extra Stickers

Extra Stickers

Extra Stickers

Extra Stickers

Extra Stickers

Extra Stickers

Extra Stickers

Extra Stickers

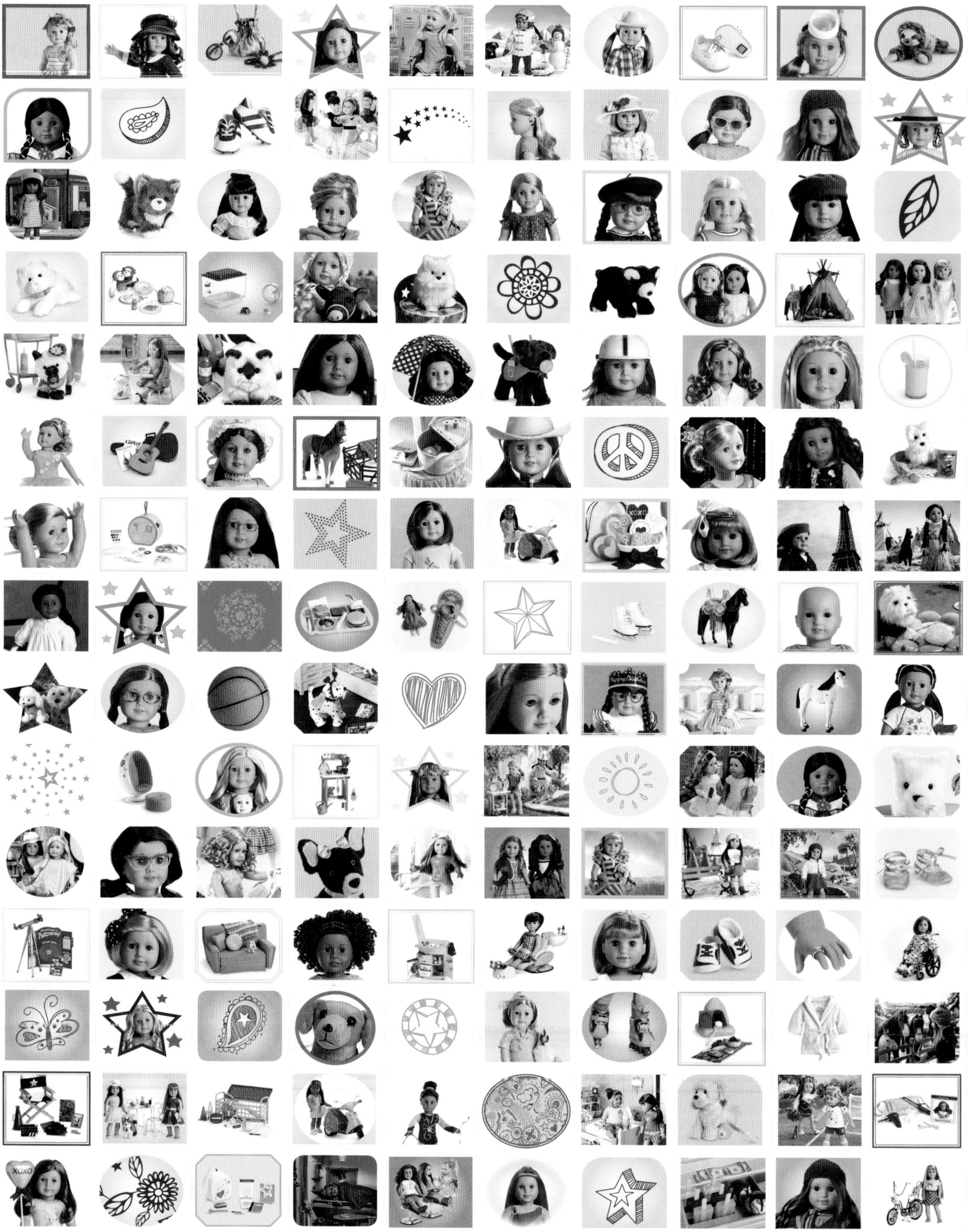

Extra Stickers

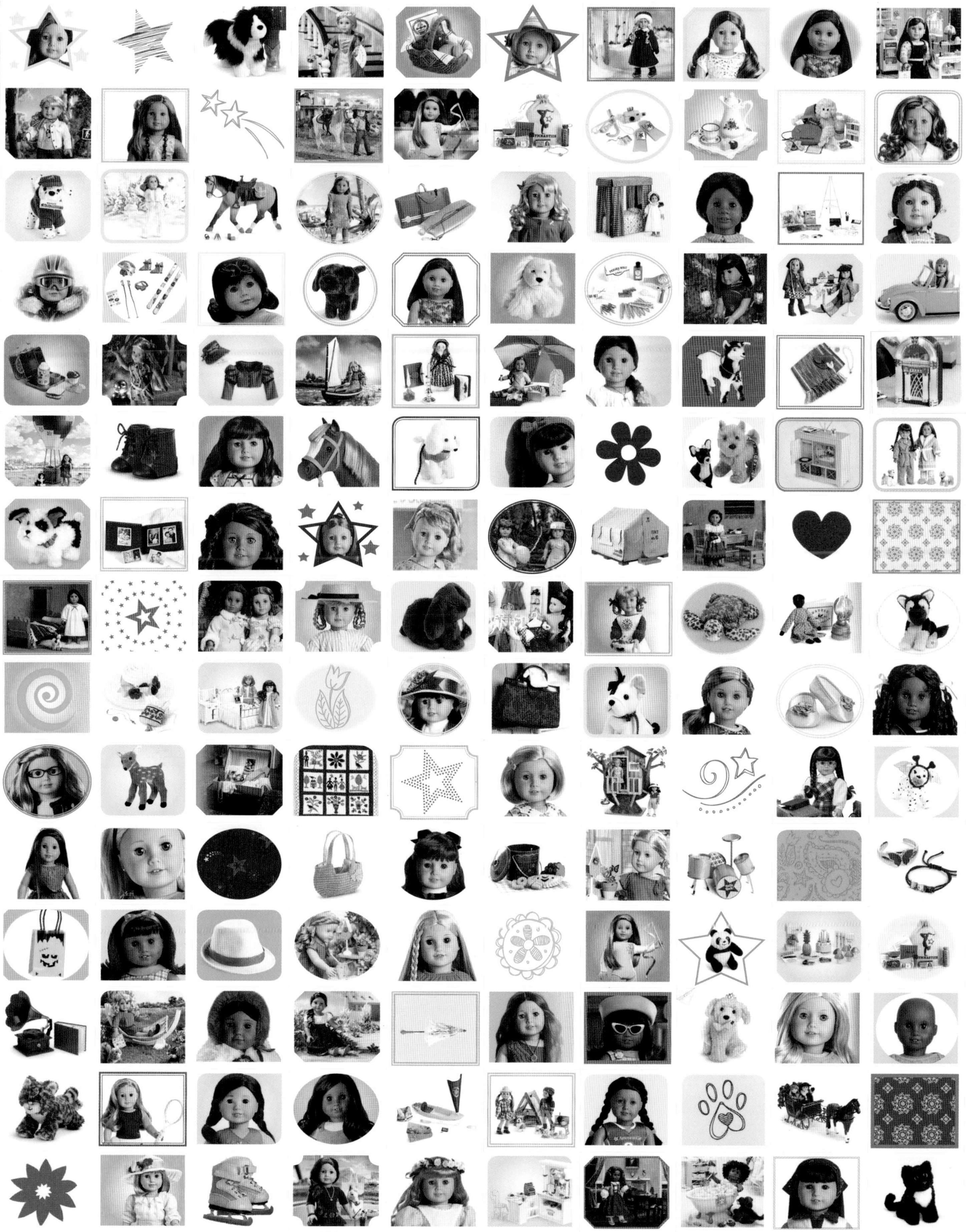